The
Wantage Tramway

by

Reg Wilkinson

THE OAKWOOD PRESS

© Oakwood Press and Reg Wilkinson 1995

First Edition published 1976
Second Enlarged Edition 1995

British Library Cataloguing in Publication Data
A Record for this book is available from the British Library
ISBN 0 85361 436 9

Typeset by Oakwood Graphics.

Printed by Henry Ling Ltd, The Dorset Press, Dorchester.

A postcard illustrating an incident in 1923, when the Wantage tram was said to have been beaten in a race with a donkey. *Author's Collection*

Published by
The Oakwood Press
P.O. Box 122, Headington, Oxford OX3 8LU

Contents

A multi-view of Wantage reproduced from a postcard of about 1905.

Introduction to the First Edition

A little over five years ago I began to take an interest in the history of Wantage and the surrounding area, and as a result I have illustrated two books and written several articles on subjects of local history. These have prompted numerous individuals to ask me for information on historic subjects peculiar to the district.

It therefore occurred to me that there was a market for inexpensive publications dealing with specialised subjects of purely local interest. Some of the things which came to mind were the Wantage Tramway, the villages of the White Horse Vale, the ancient buildings of Wantage, and the Wantage branch of the Wilts and Berks Canal.

This short history of the Wantage Tramway is therefore intended to arouse the reader's interest in an organisation which was exclusive to Wantage in the hope that he or she will delve further into its story through the books and articles published in the past.

A number of people have volunteered information or supplied the photographs on which I have based some of my illustrations. I therefore extend my thanks to Leslie Belcher; Walter Binding; H.C. Casserley; Bernard Chapman; Maurice Deane; J.A. Fleming; Miss A. Green, (County Archivist of Berkshire); R.W. Kidner; P.M. Kalla-Bishop; J. Lonsdale, (*The Times* Library); H.T. Lucy, (Publicity Manager of Amey's); Kathleen Philip; and Denis Tyler, (Editor of *Harlequin*). If I have forgotten anyone I apologise.

I am also grateful to Lyn Jones for allowing me to make use of his illustration of the Grantham Car. The original can be seen in the Wantage Museum.

This booklet is of particular interest to my wife Therese, because she remembers the tramway in its latter years and was lucky enough to take rides on the footplate of 'Jane' as a schoolgirl during World War II. I must thank her for typing the manuscript, for correcting my spelling and above all for her patience!

Reg Wilkinson,
Easter Monday, 1974.

WANTAGE STATION,   191

℈r. to THE WANTAGE TRAMWAY COMPANY, Ltd.
G.W.R. AGENTS.

NO ERROR CAN BE ADMITTED UNLESS NOTIFIED WITHIN SEVEN DAYS FROM DELIVERY OF ACCOUNT TO MR. W. NOBLE, MANAGER.

It is requested that all Cheques be crossed and made payable to the Order of the Wantage Tramway Company, Limited.

Wantage Market Place as seen from the tower of the parish church about 1910.

Author's Collection

The statue of King Alfred in Wantage Market Place about 1910.   *Author's Collection*

Introduction to Second Enlarged Edition

It was felt that the story of the Wantage Tramway Company published by Oakwood Press in 1976 should be enlarged and incorporate the many photographs that had come to light since the First Edition. With that in mind the author and myself set about updating and revising the text, with the help of Paul Towers who had collected and researched the tramway for years. We hope that you enjoy the result.

Colin Judge
1995

I would like to acknowledge the help of Mr Gordon Collier in producing photographs for this edition.

Reg Wilkinson
1995

One of the series of commercial postcards issued by Tompkins and Barrett of the Wantage Tramway. They all appear to be labelled 'The Steam Tram, Wantage', and had a brief resumé of the Tramway. *Tompkins and Barrett*

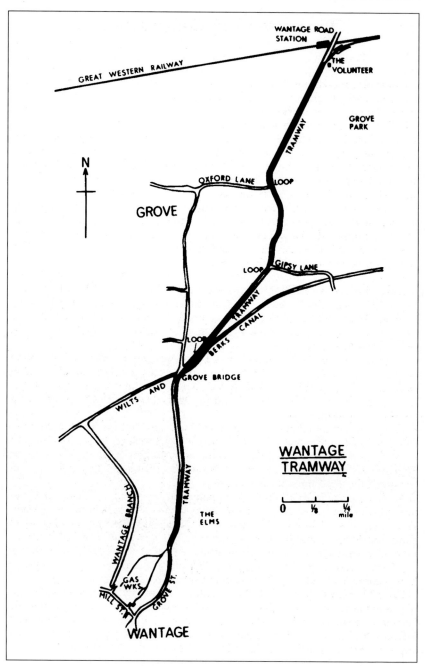

A simplified route map of the Wantage Tramway system.   *Author*

Chapter One

Promotion and Construction

Wantage, a market town nestling under the shadow of the Berkshire Downs is famous as the birthplace of King Alfred the Great; supporting a fine statue to this gentleman in the market place.

It is highly speculative that the original main line of the Great Western Railway from London to Bristol, if laid out by modern railway engineers, would have passed through or close to Wantage. But when Isambard Kingdom Brunel constructed the line in the late 1830's he naturally selected the easiest route through the White Horse Vale and as a result left Wantage (population 3,297 in the 1871 census), in isolation 2½ miles from the main line.

An attempt was made to connect the town with the railway in 1866 when the Wantage and Great Western Railway Act of 16th July, 1866 (29 & 30 Vic., cap. 231) was promoted. However, like many such branch lines the project was controlled by speculators in the City and the idea was abandoned when it failed to gain support from local businessmen.

Fortunately for the citizens of Wantage, local investors were interested in a scheme which began to gain momentum after the Tramways Act was passed in 1870. The idea was to lay a tramway along the side of the road between Wantage Town and the GWR's Wantage Road station. Initially the trams were to be horse-drawn but the promoters intended to convert them to steam power at the earliest opportunity.

A meeting 'of persons favourable to a Tramway Communication' was held in Wantage Town Hall at 'half past Three o'clock in the Afternoon' on 22nd October, 1873. Lt Col Loyd-Lindsay VC , MP , as the most active promoter of the scheme, acted as Chairman. Local residents were 'earnestly requested to assist in the undertaking'.

The Chairman said that a tramway would be a paying concern, in addition to being an asset to the town. Edward Ormond, the Solicitor, explained some of the legal issues which were involved and George Stevenson, later to be Engineer of the company, described the intended route of the tramway and explained the economics of the venture.

A resolution to form a Limited Company was passed, and a committee was formed which included the Chairman, and a dozen of the neighbourhood's best known citizens. The estimated cost of the tramway was around £9,000 and about £3,000 was subscribed at the meeting, indicating that the residents were more than willing to assist in the undertaking. It was suggested that a revenue of £4,164 would be forthcoming annually from the tramway using only five horses compared with the 25 then being used on road buses.

On 10th November, 1873 the Wantage Tramway Company Ltd was registered in accordance with the Companies' Act. Edward Ormond was made Secretary to the company and during the next nine months he worked with Edward Walmisley (a Parliamentary Agent), to get the proposed tramway approved by the Board of Trade and then authorised by Parliament.

A portrait of G. Stevenson, Engineer to the Wantage Tramway Company.

F.E.J. Burgiss

The Notice of Inaugural meeting which was displayed around Wantage
prior to the event.

Author

A Provisional order for the Wantage Tramway was passed by the Board of trade in March 1874 and it was given the Royal Assent on 7th August, 1874. The company was authorised to lay a tramway from its connection with the Great Western Railway at Wantage Road station to Wantage Market Place, running along the eastern side of the Besselsleigh Road with provision for sidings, junctions and crossing loops as required.

The length of the line was 2 miles, 38 chains with 2 miles of this laying on public roads. Five chains were double track and five passing loops were authorised. The entire line was constructed to the standard gauge of 4 ft 8½ in. A rough estimate of the constructional cost came to about £7,500, with a further £1,100 for the suggested rolling stock of 2 horses with 2 passenger cars, 2 trucks and an engine.

Shortly after the Royal Assent was granted the Directors sought tenders for the line with the following advertisement:

The Wantage Tramway Company Ltd will receive tenders for constructing a single line of a tramway for the distance of about 2¼ miles by the side of the Turnpike Road between the town of Wantage and Wantage Road Station (GWR). Plans and specifications can be seen at the office of Mr G. Stevenson (Engineer) Wantage, to whom Tenders are to be sent on or before the 15th September next.

Wantage, 20th August, 1874

The following tenders were received:

Name of Contractor	Address	Amount of Tender		
George Young	2 Britannia Villa, Albion Gardens, Hammersmith	£8,500	0	0
Michael Duffy and James Crutchley	(Office) 132 Fenchurch Street, London	£8,200	0	0
I.M. Wiswell	31 Lower Sackville Street, Dublin	£7,000	0	0
John Coker*	Chale, Isle of Wight	£6,620	0	0
R.W. Fitzmaurice & Co.	Pavin, Wharf, Morville, Street, Birmingham	£6,200	0	0
Thomas Wainwright & Co.	14 Shrubland Road, Dalston, London	£6,150	0	0
Allen Vickers	7 Radcot Street, Kennington, London, S.E.	£5,975	0	0
Joseph Rendell	1 Ottway Street, Lower Clapton, London, N.	£5,626	0	0
John Wilkinson	Nottingham	£5,350	0	0
Philip Ward	Salop Row, Handsworth, Birmingham	£4,201	0	0

* John Coker stated that he had been the contractor for the Ryde Tramway, Isle of Wight.

The tenders were discussed at the Board meeting of 16th September, 1874. Philip Ward of Birmingham was the lowest and a formal agreement was signed

A fine close-up view of the ornate front of the Mill Street office building, showing the use of coloured bricks and terracotta to great aesthetic advantage.

Author

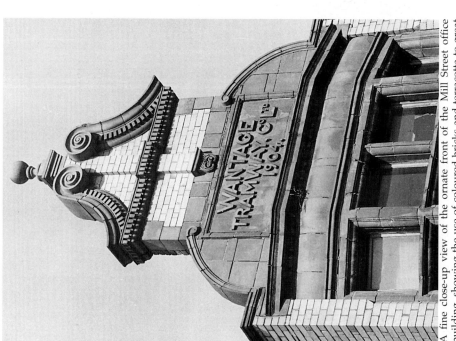

Another view of the Tramway's office building, looking down Mill Street.

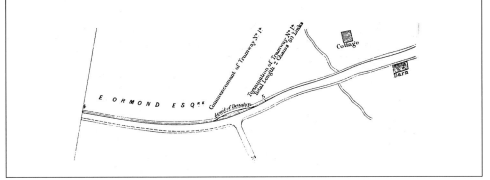

The original survey for the passing loop cum station at Oxford Lane (the first stopping place after the GWR Wantage Road terminus).

Continuation of the above showing the tramway passing Grove Farm with the Challow Lane coming into the main road.

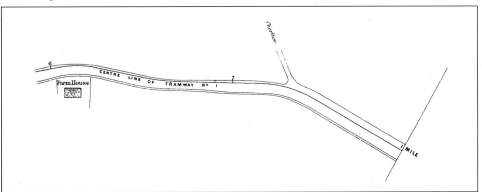

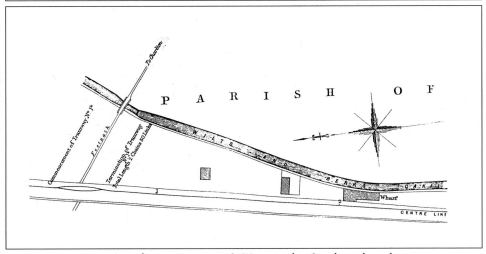

Again continuing along the tramway towards Wantage, the plan shows how the tramway ran alongside the Wilts and Berks Canal with the cottages at the wharf clearly shown.

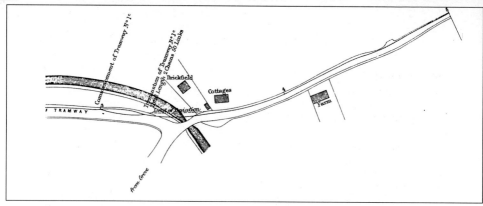

Further on towards Wantage the tramway crossed the Wilts and Berks Canal. This was the major engineering feature of the tramway. The canal company charged £100 just for the right to cross the canal and the bridge was estimated to cost £250 to build.

The original plan showing the terminus in the Market Place, next to the Town Hall, Wantage. This proposal was rejected owing to the steep rise from Mill Street up into the Market Place.

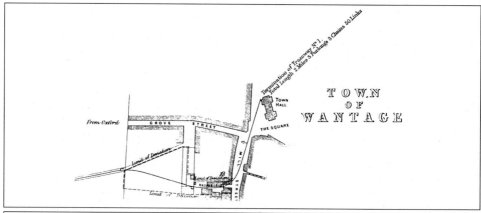

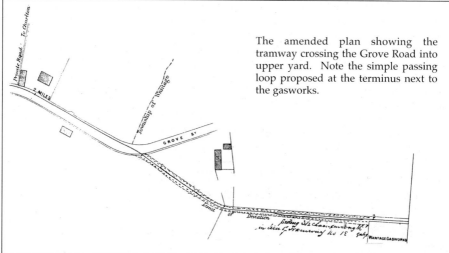

The amended plan showing the tramway crossing the Grove Road into upper yard. Note the simple passing loop proposed at the terminus next to the gasworks.

with him on 9th December, 1874.

Construction of the line was started immediately in December 1874 and was comparatively uneventful, taking about eight months to complete. Instead of carrying on the line to the Market Place it was decided to terminate the line in Mill Street and build a small station (at a later date). Several old houses were demolished to make way for the approach road and platform, with a station house, (built by a local builder Whiting and Tosland). The platform having a roof of curved corrugated iron some 50 ft in span and 19 ft deep (this being rebuilt in 1890).

The track rails were of a bridge section of 40lb. and bolted to longitudinal timbers 6 in. x 10 in. in section. The transoms, which were beneath the sleepers, were 4 in. x 5 in. in section and spaced at ten foot intervals. Only the steel girder bridge of 38 ft width over the Wilts and Berks Canal near Grove caused any concern to the Engineer.

The first horse-drawn tramcar arrived at Wantage in the summer of 1875 and Col C.S. Hutchinson, the Board of Trade Inspector, travelled in it, accompanied by the Directors of the Tramway company, to carry out an inspection of the line on 26th August.

A few minor alterations were recommended, but otherwise the tramway satisfied all the necessary requirements and a Board of Trade certificate to that effect was issued four days later.

The line was opened for goods traffic on 1st October, 1875 and for passenger traffic 10 days later. At that time there was only one horse-drawn tramcar (the Starbuck Tramcar No. 1), at Wantage and because of this the advertised timetable was maintained with the help of Nunney's horse drawn omnibus. When in December, a second tramcar (No. 2) became available the Tramway Company took over Mr Nunney's public service to Wantage Road station. He was paid £100 for the goodwill, and the take-over included his parcel agency to the GWR.

Horse tramcar No. 1 had arrived at Wantage in August 1875 direct from the Starbuck Car and Wagon Company of Clevedon Street, Birkenhead, closely followed in December 1875 by car No. 2. Both of these cars had first and second class accommodation and had the unusual feature of being constructed with leaf springs and railway axle boxes.

Tramcar No. 1 was constructed as a double-decked vehicle fitted with back to back knife-board seating, whereas vehicle No. 2 was a single-deck tramcar. Within five years car No. 1 was converted to a single-deck vehicle. When steam power was introduced, these vehicles were used as passengers coaches and their details are dealt with in *Chapter Three*.

WANTAGE—*Berkshire.*

GIBBONS, P. & H. P., Vale of White. Horse Iron Works.

steam engines —— machines à vapeur —— Dampfma-schinen.

NALDER & NALDER, Challow Iron Works.

threshing machines——machines à battre les blés—— Dreschmaschinen.

The entry for 1876 from the *Directory of Manufacturers* showing just two entries for the town.

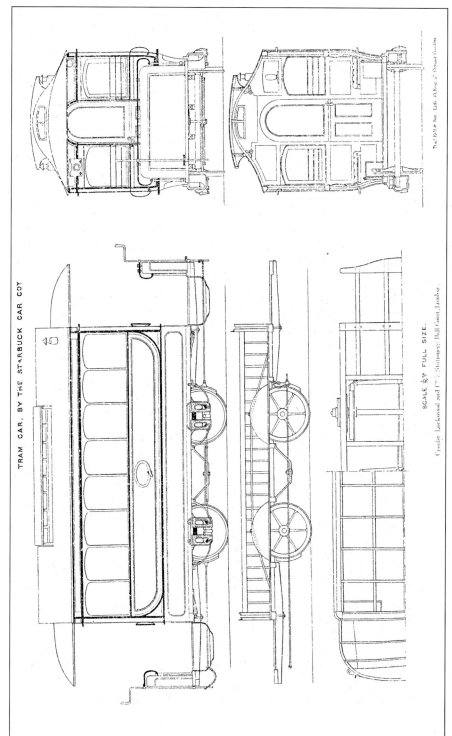

TRAM CAR, BY THE STARBUCK CAR COY.

SCALE $\frac{3}{4}$ FULL SIZE.

An official drawing of a tram car designed by the Starbuck Car Co. which was very similar to the Wantage cars.

Chapter Two

Introduction of Steam Power

At the turn of the year the tramway was running smoothly and the company's Directors decided that they could turn their attention to the procurement of a reliable steam-driven tramway engine. With this idea in mind Edward Ormond and George Stevenson had already inspected John Grantham's Steam Car more than a year earlier on 25th September, 1874. Both considered it suitable for use on the tramway, and it was moved to Wantage for trials during the summer of 1875.

The Parliamentary Order which gave the permission for the construction and operation of the Tramway allowed only for the use of animal traction. Because of this, the trials of the Grantham car had to take place on that part of the line which ran between Grove Road and the Wantage Mill Street terminus. As this section of the tramway was on company property and well away from the public highway, the Board of Trade could raise no objections. The Grantham steam tramcar was designed in 1872 by John Grantham (1809-1894) to compete in trials for the Howard Medal. This prodigious award was offered by the Society of Arts for the design of a traction engine which would be suitable as a substitute for horse power on tramways. One of the conditions was that the engine had to be contained within the vehicle which carried the passengers. Grantham's car fulfilled this requirement and for this reason was described as a 'Combined Steam Tramcar'.

Its construction consisted of an ordinary four-wheeled double decked car in the centre of which were steam boiler chambers, each of which contained a small vertical boiler constructed on the Field system(18 in. in diameter and 4 ft 4 in. high). The compartments were separated from each other by a corridor, open to the inside of the vehicle at each end so that there was no obstruction between the driver, conductor and the passengers. The power plant (laying under the floor) consisted of two cylinders 4 in. in diameter with a 10 in. stroke, driving a single pair of 30 in. diameter wheels.

Grantham entrusted the design of his vehicle to Merryweather & Co. of London, whilst the bodywork was carried out by the Oldbury Carriage & Wagon Works near Birmingham. The steam car had only four wheels which were placed on a 10 ft wheelbase. Only one axle was used for driving the vehicle; the other axle had one loose wheel (on a sleeve) so that the wheels could revolve independently of each other. Its overall length was 30 ft; it had 44 passenger seats (20 inside the lower deck and 24 outside on top). These upper deck seats were of the knifeboard type and were placed along the length of the clerestory. Access to the top deck was by means of a primitive iron ladder at each end; the total weight of the vehicle was 6½ tons.

Early in 1873, the steam car was put to work experimentally on a short length of level track (350 yards in length) at West Brompton in London where it performed satisfactorily for some time, traversing the line at an average speed of 11 miles per hour on a boiler pressure of 90 lbs. In November of the same

Three views of the Grantham Steam Car with the bottom view on this page showing the side panels lowered to allow access to the motion and cylinders. *Courtesy Science Museum*

year, further runs were carried out along Vauxhall Bridge Road on the London Tramway system but these trials proved unsatisfactory due to the grit and debris in the grooved track.

The car was then moved to the Wantage Tramway but initially proved to be unsuitable for the job required. Between September 1875 and June 1876 the vehicle was extensively rebuilt with the two original Merryweather boilers being replaced by a single Shand, Mason and Co. boiler. This improved the steam pressure and enabled the vehicle to accomplish the steep climb to the Wantage terminus without the numerous failures previously encountered. At the same time the wheels were reduced to 24 in. diameter, and the vehicle dimensions were reduced to 27 ft 3 in. in length, 6 ft 6 in. wide and 11 ft 1 in. high, but with an increased weight of 8 tons. It was now capable of carrying 60 passengers and was still able to be driven from either end.

During the trials, Col Loyd-Lindsay, Edward Ormond and Edward Walmisley were working behind the scenes to obtain permission for the use of mechanical traction on the tramway. After a number of setbacks the Parliamentary Order, authorising the company to operate the Wantage Tramway by steam or any other mechanical means was finally approved by the Royal Assent on 27th June, 1876. The Grantham car made several experimental runs along the whole length of the tramway on the evening of the 5th July, 1876, the last one of the day being a free trip to anyone wishing to travel. More than 100 passengers made the journey to the GWR station at Wantage Road and back and were greeted by cheering crowds at Mill Street. The Directors, passengers and onlookers all declared that they were in favour of the 'new fangled' steam vehicle as the method of traction.

The Grantham car was placed in regular service without ceremony on 1st August, 1876 and the Wantage Tramway became the very first tramway in Britain to operate a passenger service using steam traction. On 18th September, 1876, Robert Baxter (representing the owners of the vehicle) was paid £250 for the car and an addition of £37 for the installation of the new Shand boiler.

John Grantham died in July 1874 (at the age of 65) so regrettably did not live to see his invention perform the job it was intended for. However his work did not go unrecognised because the Council of the Society of Arts awarded the Howard Medal to him posthumously; this was presented to his widow in April 1875.

This vehicle lasted for nearly 15 years and during that time was the only self-propelled passenger vehicle at work on the tramway. It was withdrawn in 1890 and sold for scrap (to the value of 76 shillings - just under £4) in 1891.

Whilst working on the tramway the following annual costs were estimated for the vehicle:

					£	s	d
1 engine driver	@	35s.	per week				
1 stoker	@	25s.	per week	80s.	208	0	0
1 conductor	@	20s.	per week				
Fuel, 7lb. coke per mile for 26,260 miles = 82 tons @ 15s.					61	10	0
Oil, tallow, wash, and sundries, @ ¼d. per mile, for 26,260 miles					27	7	1
Water at 1s. per day					18	5	0
Repairs of car and machinery, at 1d. per mile, for 26,260 miles					109	8	4
TOTAL COST					£424	10	5
or 3.88d. per mile-run.							

Chapter Three

Building up the Rolling Stock

Locomotives (Part One)

In November 1876 a second steam tram engine arrived at Wantage. This again had been built by Merryweather & Sons of Lambeth under the patents of James Compton Merryweather (dated April 1875) and its purchase price was £500, if found satisfactory after the trial period.

This tram engine and the Grantham steam car were inspected by Col Hutchinson on 25th November, 1876 and as a result the latter vehicle was despatched to the Avonside Engine Company, Bristol for modifications to comply with the current Board of Trade regulations. In the absence of the Grantham car, the Merryweather engine had to work the passenger service. Unfortunately the vehicle did not come up to the Directors' expectations and in early 1877 it was returned to the makers (in a rather dilapidated state) after standing idle for many months in Wantage terminus yard. This particular engine was worked on a boiler pressure of 120psi using a locomotive style boiler (fired at the side) and through a Stephenson's Link motion to a single axle with a belt drive to a governor which controlled the maximum speed to 10 mph.

The Grantham car arrived back at Wantage in March 1877 and in the same month another steam tram engine was put on trial. This was built by Henry Hughes & Co. of Loughborough and could be driven from either end. This vehicle was built as an 0-4-0 but it usually ran as a 2-2-0, except in severe weather conditions or when working heavy goods trains. The Directors had hoped that this would be powerful enough to handle the increasing goods traffic. The load that was required to be hauled by this engine was two 10-ton trucks at an average speed of 6 mph. After the trial on the 19th April, 1877, proving that it was not capable of this performance, the Hughes engine was put to work on regular passenger service. Later during the year it was returned to the factory at Loughborough for minor modifications but by September 1877 the company purchased it for £600.

This was then the first engine to be owned by the tramway company. By January 1895 it was in a very sorry state and the GWR Works at Swindon was asked to give it a thorough overhaul (including a new boiler). According to the records, this engine was worked quite hard, making eight return trips daily, each trip performed in 32 minutes or an average speed of 9.4 mph, and using about 300lb. of coal per day and hauling, on average, about 6½ tons per trip. She was withdrawn in 1919 and officially scrapped in 1920.

The search for a suitable goods engine continued as in 1875 the Directors minuted the following;

We are enquiring for a small steam engine with which to convey heavy traffic to and from the station and do not recommend the purchase of cart horses for this purpose.

As Tramways in general were constructed mainly to accommodate passenger

A typical Merryweather 0-4-0 tram steam engine, this particular model being a company demonstration engine.   *Courtesy Science Museum*

A view of Wantage Tramway engine No. 4.   *Real Photographs*

WANTAGE TWY.

Nº 4

BUILT HUGHES 1877

This drawing by Colin Binnie and supplied by Paul Towers is based on photographic evidence and in particular the photograph on the previous page. The wheel diameter was known to be 2 ft 6 in. and the wheelbase was 4 ft.

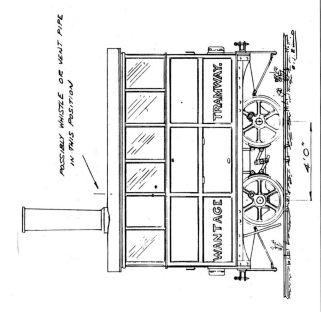

POSSIBLY WHISTLE OR VENT PIPE IN THIS POSITION

TRAMWAY.

WANTAGE

4' 0"

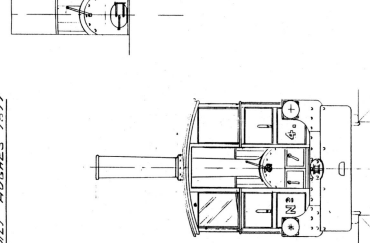

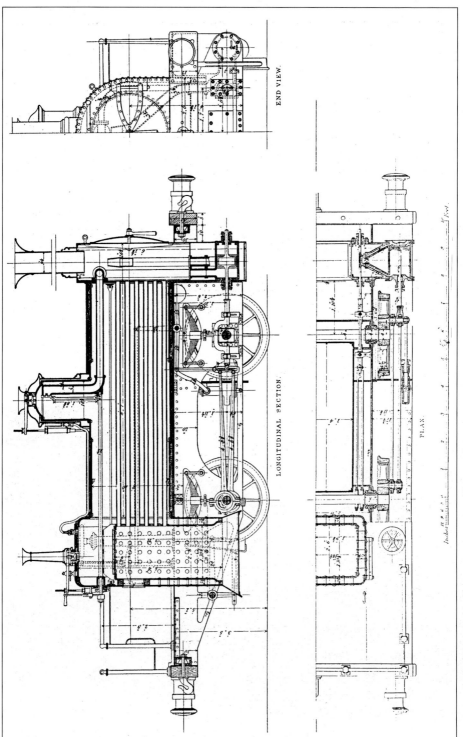

END VIEW.

LONGITUDINAL SECTION.

PLAN.

Official working drawing of No. 5 (later *Shannon*) as built by George England & Co. Ltd, London, for the Sandy & Potton Railway.

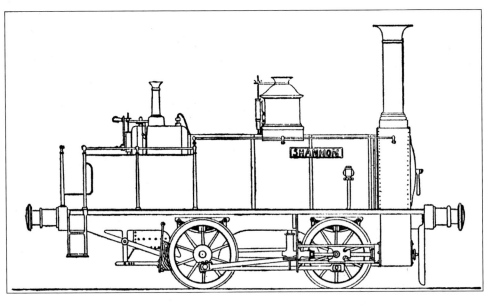

A side view of *Shannon* as built.

This early view of No. 5 (nicknamed 'Jane' by the tramway) previously named *Shannon*, standing on the shed road (also the entry to the gasworks sidings) at Wantage upper yard. The engine is seen here with a Swindon copper capped chimney and steel plate affixed to the buffer beam.   *Real Photographs*

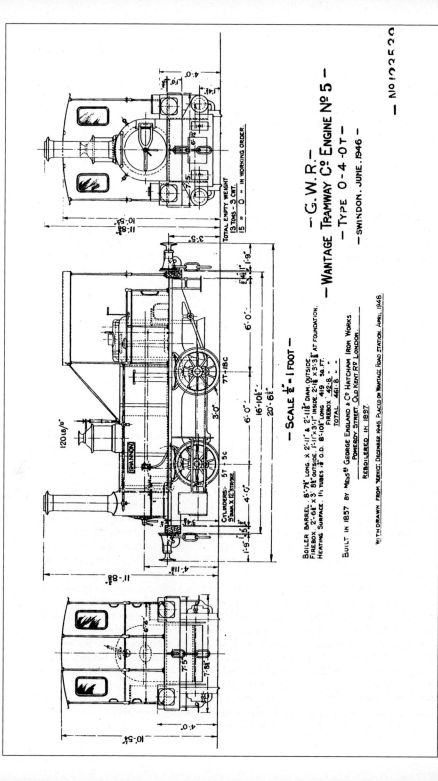

The official Swindon GWR works drawing.

traffic, the lack of suitable goods engines for tramways was not surprising.

During 1876, the Board considered the plans and specification for a 0-4-0 locomotive from the Shand & Mason Company but postponed a decision until a later date. The LNWR Company at Crewe sent a specification of surplus locomotives they had on offer to Wantage on 5th January, 1878:

One 4-wheeled coupled, currently at work within these Works and one 6-wheeled engine not coupled.

The 0-4-0 was on offer for £350 but as William Dean also wrote from Swindon stating that the GWR had an Avonside 0-6-0, built in 1871, available for £500, the directors were now in a dilemma as to the choice.

However, after a long and successful inspection by a Mr Daniel Young of Witney (who charged £7 13s. 0d. for his services), the Directors decided to make an offer to the LNWR for No. 1863, but the reply received from Mr F.W. Webb at Crewe was not what they expected. The latter stated that when the LNWR fixed a price for an item they had for sale that was the figure they wanted and offers were not required! In addition, as the Wantage Tramway had dragged its feet in making a reply the locomotive in question was being purchased by another party. However, after hurried consultations a cheque was dispatched for £365 8s. 1d. in May 1878 and *Shannon* (under her own steam) was moved from Crewe to Oxford. An agreement with the GWR allowed *Shannon* to transfer to the GWR metals at Oxford and continue her journey, again under her own steam, to Wantage Road station.

The engine was built in 1857 by George England & Co., Hatcham Ironworks, New Cross, London as a well tank 0-4-0 with wheel diameters of 2 ft 10½ in. and cylinders 9¼ in. x 12 in., for the proprietor Capt. William Peel, RN of the Sandy and Potton Railway and cost £800. In 1862 the locomotive was sold to the LNWR, together with all other assets of the railway, for £20,000. She was numbered 1104 in the LNWR's duplicate list and put on trial in 1862 on the Cromford and High Peak Railway (C&HPR). This trial only lasted for two weeks as the engine did not perform too well on the steep gradients and tortuous curves of the C&HPR. On return to Crewe she was employed on works and local station duties and renumbered in 1872 to LNWR No. 1863.

Soon after arriving at Wantage she was officially known as No. 5 and occasionally referred to as 'Jane' but never carried this name. The original name of *Shannon* had been carried for about six years whilst in LNWR service, the name being affixed by its first owner, Capt. Peel, as a tribute to the 50 gun steam frigate under his command. During her service with Wantage Tramway, the locomotive was little altered and according to the records, never received a new boiler, although new cylinders were fitted in 1882. In 1896 she went to the Swindon Works for heavy repairs and, in early 1921 (again at Swindon), received new tube plates, new tubes and back plate, plus steam brakes, being returned to service on 7th March, 1921. After the overhaul, No. 5 often ran 65 miles per day, making 12 return trips. During 1922, No. 5 seemed to have caused problems for the traffic department as it is recorded as having been derailed six times; smashed a motor vehicle, a horse and cart, and a bullock plus

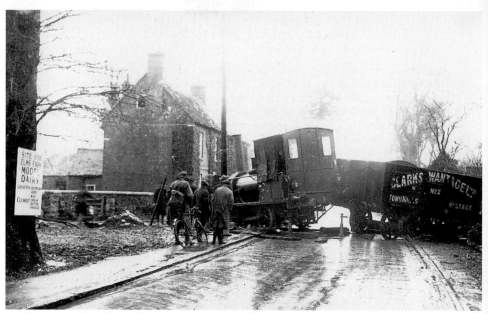

The scene of No. 5's accident on the rainy day of 8th January, 1936; driver Jack Vincent had been at the controls. It was reported that 'Jane' left the rails due to a brick lying in the track, and blocked the road completely for about 12 hours. Note the board acclaiming the site for the new Elms Farm Dairy; this view also gives a good side-on look at Private Owner wagon No. 2 for Clark's Mill in Wantage. *Author's Collection*

This later view (in the late 1930s) of No. 5 shows the chimney cap removed, the steel plates gone, the buffers changed to a lighter type, the handrails changed and lamp brackets and standard couplings added. *H.C. Casserley*

other minor infringements - some record for one engine!

In 1929 she left Wantage once again but this time to the Avonside Engine Co. at Bristol for a 'general overhaul', returning in February 1930.

On 8th January, 1936, whilst hauling five trucks from Wantage, No. 5 derailed near to Grove Bridge blocking the road as shown in the accompanying photograph. It took the staff until 11 am the next day to re-open the road to motor traffic. In 1939 a further overhaul at the GWR Swindon Works saw No. 5 being repainted in green with the lettering 'W. T. Co. No. 5' painted in yellow on the cabside and a works plate carrying the words 'Registered by GWR No. 209, 1941'.

On the 25th April, 1946 (after closure of the tramway) the GWR purchased the locomotive *Shannon* for £100 at the clearance sale. They moved her (coupled into a goods train) to Swindon in May and then overhauled her yet again, the work also including repainting and adding nameplates to the boiler with the name *Shannon*.

After a meeting at Swindon it was decided that a fitting resting place for the engine would be on the platform at Wantage Road GWR station where she was placed in 1948. A plaque was attached to the display for all to see.

In the July 1946 issue of the *Great Western Railway Magazine* the following poem which had been written by Mr J.M. Scott of Glasgow was included.

Where Shannon Goes

Only an engine, small, decrepit, old,
Way-worn with years and with its duty done,
Still on the heart its captivations hold,
And now at last a resting-place hath won,
Thanks to *The Times* whose Leader held the day
With words that raptur'd young and old alike,
The plume of steam and that onrushing way
That stays the steps of even those who hike.
The rural scene, the yet far-distant sound,
The overbridge that gains the instant view,
The nearing speck that is no sooner found
Than in a flash is but as distant too!
This, then, its theme and that now long ago
The "Shannon" knew and its proud lineage tells,
When life was leisured as the Shannon's flow
And coach and four still cast their ancient spells.
Now (like its namesake) it will honoured be,
If not in song, at least in story told;
A monument rather than a memory
Such tales in telling never do grow old.

Unfortunately in 1965 the former GWR station at Wantage Road was closed as a result of the infamous 'Beeching Plan' and yet again the fate of No. 5 *Shannon* hung in the balance. Through the efforts of Mervyn Scott (then Chairman of the Wantage Urban District Council) the Town Council agreed to obtain funds to renovate the locomotive and place it on display somewhere in Wantage. It was estimated that around £2,000 would be needed to carry out the

A good front view of No. 5 standing at the GWR Wantage Road site. *LCGB Collection*

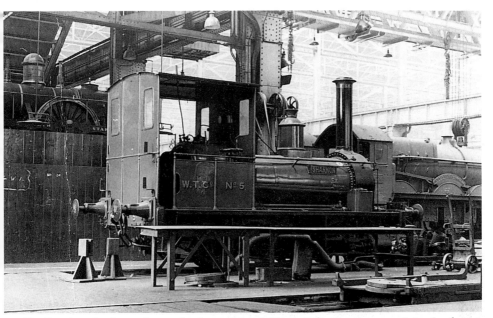

No. 5 undergoing her major overhaul, repaint and fitting of the *Shannon* nameplates, by the Great Western Railway in July 1947, under the gaze of the broad gauge engine *North Star*. Note the 'Castle' class 4-6-0 No. 4076 *Carmarthen Castle* undergoing its major overhaul in the background.   *H.C. Casserley*

The finished result seen here by the official works photographer outside Swindon Works (the background has been painted out).   *GWR*

The modern concrete enclosure put up for No. 5 on the platform of the GWR station at Wantage Road, photographed here in 1948. *Howard Evans*

Seen from the footbridge over the main line at Wantage Road station is a further view of *Shannon* in its specially constructed enclosure, photographed in 1959. *H.C. Casserley*

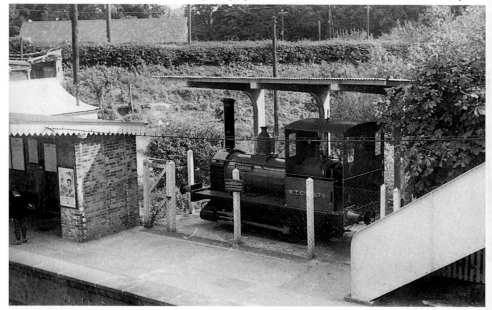

The plaque which was attached to the enclosure at Wantage Road.   *Author*

The final removal from the Wantage Road station in November 1966 of No. 5 (ex-*Shannon*) prior
to travelling to the Wantage Radiation Laboratories at Grove. Her nameplates were removed
and never returned, she was now just 'No. 5'.   *Author's Collection*

Two early views at the Wantage terminus of No. 7 in its original form with the cab very much open to the elements. Both sides of the locomotive are shown. *Real Photographs*

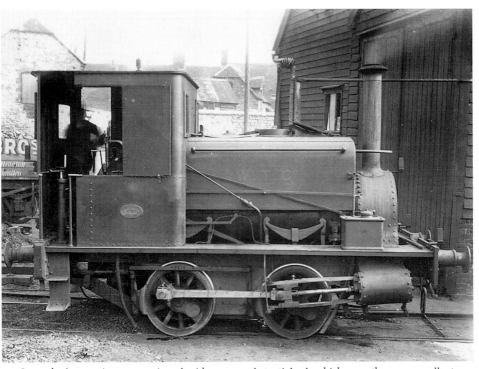

Later the locomotive was equipped with a very substantial cab which gave the crew excellent protection from the elements and here we see No. 7 in the 1920s at the Wantage terminus, Upper Yard. *Real Photographs and A.W. Croughton*

No. 7 seen here on her visit to the GWR Swindon Works in 1924. *Real Photographs*

No. 7 in the lower yard, 11th October, 1930. *Dr. Jack Hollick/Adrian Vaughan Collection*

of monies spent should be kept as well as authorising the replacement of its wheels. However by the November of 1883, the following sale notice appeared;

Sale of an engine at Wantage Road on the GWR (near Swindon) Upset price £250. Messrs. W and S. Hern will sell by auction at Wantage Road Station (GWR) near Swindon on Wednesday the 28th November, at 1.30 pm . . . a new Patent Tramway, Tip or Bank Engine, 4 ft 8½ in. gauge. 'Locomotive Type', 6¼ in. cylinders, 10 in. stroke, copper firebox, built under special supervision of the very best materials at a cost of £900.
The engine fulfils all the requirements of the Board of Trade for Street tramway engines and can be driven from either end, a special feature of the machine being that its working parts are enclosed from dust and dirt, thus saving at least 40 per cent in wear and tear. The engine is now running on the Wantage Tramway (Wantage Road GWR). Photograph and model can be seen and reports and further particulars obtained of the Auctioneers, 72 St Mary's Street, Cardiff.

Regrettably no prospective buyers appeared and so the engine remained unused in the Wantage Yard. However in 1888 the company purchased No. 6 for just £60 (the cheapest locomotive they acquired) and in 1909, the GWR provided a new boiler. In 1922 a new steel firebox was made by a local firm, Nalder & Nalder of Challow. She was finally withdrawn in 1925 and sold for scrap to W.G. Keen & Co. of Bristol and subsequently broken up at Wantage Road yard in 1931. Her specifications were 2-2-0 wheel arrangement with 2 ft 4 in. diameter wheels on a 4 ft 6 in. wheel base, the locomotive weighing 11 tons and working with a steam pressure of 140psi.

After No. 6 came one of the most successful engines the Wantage Tramway ever possessed. This was No. 7, purchased in 1893 for £300. Built in 1888 to Works No. 1057 by the Manning, Wardle Company Ltd of Leeds, it was one of 139 engines built over a period of 52 years, to the company's standard class 'F' contractor designs. This particular locomotive (named *Massey*) was one of a series supplied in March 1888 to T.A. Walker, who was at the time working on the Manchester Ship Canal Contract. The Works' delivery book states that she was steamed and then despatched to Ince. Once established on the Wantage Tramway the engine proved to be very useful and a great success. The Company fitted a large overall cab (the previous fixture only had a front and rear weather board for protection). This locomotive was never named on the Wantage Tramway and was known officially as No. 7. In 1900, Swindon Works fitted a new boiler and in 1921 it was described as being totally rebuilt, again at the GWR Works. Later in 1924, it spent five more months at Swindon but the reason for this is not recorded.

No. 7 lasted until the line closed; being the only workable engine available in the final years of operation. In 1946, after working the demolition trains, she was finally sold to A.R. Adams of Newport, Wales, for the princely sum of £205, being transported to Newport by road. It was apparently used in Cordes Steel Mills Ltd until 1956 when yet again it was offered for sale but no takers were forthcoming and the engine was subsequently broken-up.

The dimensions for No. 7 were: cylinders 10 in. x 14 in. stroke with 2 ft 9 in. diameter wheels; the engine had a 4 ft 9 in. wheelbase and a working pressure

1329·1330·1331·1332·1333

Sold 1909 to Powlesland & Mason 1909

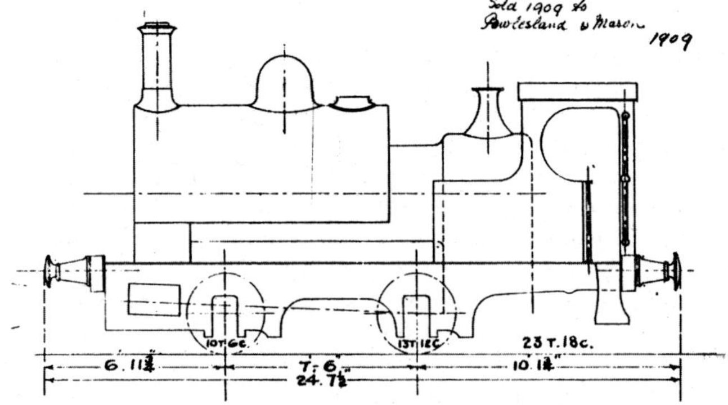

10T 6C.
13T 12C.
23 T. 18C.
6. 11¾
7. 6
10. 1¼
24. 7½

DESCRIPTION

CYLINDERS	Diam. 14" Stroke 18 Steam Ports 1.0" × 1" Exhaust 1.0" × 2½"
BOILER	Barrel. Diam Outside 3. 6⅞ Length 8. 11"
FIREBOX	Outside 3.6" × 3. 8½" Inside 3. 0⅞ × 3. 3¼" Height 4. 10¾
TUBES	No. 197 Diam. 1¾ Length 10. 3
HEATING SURFACE	Tubes 923·8 sq ft Firebox 62·79 sq. ft. Total 986·5 sq. ft.
AREA OF FIREGRATE	9' 9" sq. ft
WHEELS	Diam 3. 0.
WATER CAPACITY OF TANK.	700 Gallons
WORKING PRESSURE	150 Lbs

1359
"WYE"

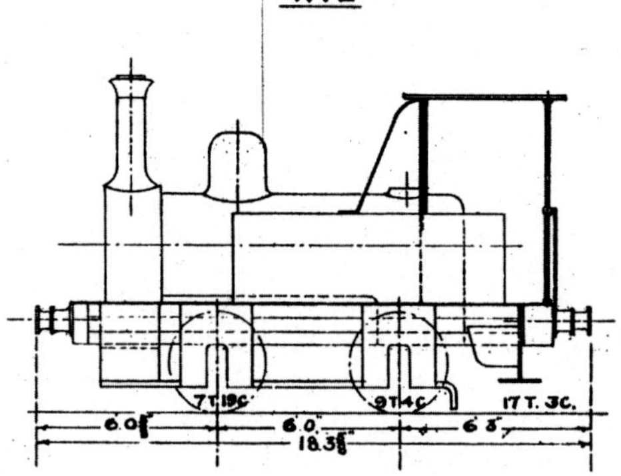

7T. 19C
9T. 4C
17 T. 3C.
6. 0⅝
6. 0.
6 3
18. 3⅝

DESCRIPTION

CYLINDERS	Diam 10" Stroke 20" Steam Ports 7 × 1" Exhaust 7 × .
BOILER	Barrel. Diam. Outside Length 7. 2¼"
FIREBOX	Outside 2. 10 × 3. 3¼ Inside 2. 2¼ × 2. 6¾ Height 3. 6"
TUBES	No 121 Diam. 1½" Length 7. 5⅝
HEATING SURFACE	Tubes 354 sq. ft. Firebox 35 sq. ft. Total 389 sq. ft.
AREA OF FIREGRATE	5·6 sq. ft.
WHEELS	Diam. 3. 3"
WATER CAPACITY OF TANK.	330 Gallons
WORKING PRESSURE	120 Lbs

of 125psi and weighed 14 tons 15 cwt (bunker capacity 15 cwt).

By 1909 the company had decided that it needed more motive power and approached the ever faithful GWR for a suitable locomotive. After months of negotiation they finally purchased GWR No. 1329 in March 1910. This locomotive was an ex-South Devon Railway 0-4-0 outside cylinder, saddle tank, built by the Avonside Engine Co. Ltd in November 1874 to Works No. 1052. Eight of this class were constructed for the South Devon Rly. and all named after animals or birds this one being constructed as a broad gauge (7 ft) locomotive and numbered 2175 (named *Raven*), she was converted to standard gauge in 1892. The principal dimensions were 14 in. cylinders and 18 in. stroke, driving 3 ft diameter wheels on a 7 ft 6 in. wheelbase. Boiler pressure was 150psi and the working weight was 23 tons 18 cwt. The engine had seen service on the Torbay and Brixham Railway before being absorbed into the GWR. Because of its weight and its long wheelbase, the engine was really unsuitable for tramway use, particularly as it was mounted on volute springs, making it very sensitive to the bad and uneven trackwork it encountered on the Wantage Tramway. Reports say that while hauling 17 wagons it became derailed due to a broken wheel flange whereupon it was hauled to the lower yard to lay derelict until it was eventually scrapped in 1919.

The tramway encountered a serious problem in 1906 when locomotive No. 7 burst a cylinder. Whilst No. 7 was at Swindon Works for repairs the company hired a 0-4-0 side tank GWR No. 1359, named *Wye* at 3 shillings per day with a minimum charge of £1 per week. The locomotive arrived at Wantage minus its nameplate. This engine was a former Severn & Wye Railway locomotive built by Fletcher, Jennings and Co. Ltd of Whitehaven around 1876 (works No. 153), it being absorbed into the GWR in 1894.

Soon after arrival at Wantage, the GWR offered the Tramway company the chance to purchase No. 1359 for £300. Hard negotiations forced the price down to £250 and the company eventually offered £200, but the locomotive remained in the ownership of the GWR until its withdrawal in 1910.

The last locomotive the Tramway company acquired (during the summer of 1919) was bought by tender from the Royal Arsenal at Woolwich for the sum of £600. It arrived at Wantage Road on a GWR Crocodile Truck and this was hauled along the tramway into the Lower Yard for it to be unloaded. Apparently it was bought without any consideration for a cautionary engineer's report and although steamed easily was useless in maintaining any working pressure. One old driver stated; 'She was only a good engine as long as she was standing still'. Apparently a cracked cylinder was to blame but this was only found when the locomotive was broken up.

Named the *Driver* by the Tramway company, it reputedly once carried the name *The Gunner* whilst at Woolwich. She was a class 'H', Manning, Wardle 0-4-0 tank with 2 ft 9 in. diameter wheels with cylinders of 12 in. dia. and a stroke of 18 in. being supplied to Woolwich (new) on 25th January, 1875. By 1920 this engine was being broken up at Wantage, having survived less than a year.

In 1919-20, the company desperately needed a workable goods locomotive and as new locomotives were hard to come by after the Great War, second-hand

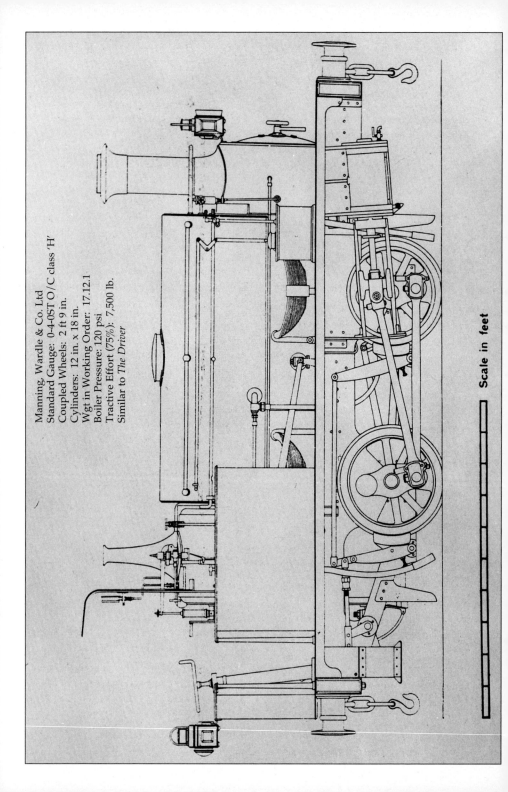

Manning, Wardle & Co. Ltd
Standard Gauge: 0-4-0ST O/C class 'H'
Coupled Wheels: 2 ft 9 in.
Cylinders: 12 in. x 18 in.
Wgt in Working Order: 17.12.1
Boiler Pressure: 120 psi
Tractive Effort (75%): 7,500 lb.
Similar to *The Driver*

Scale in feet

examples were having to be considered. In May 1920, the company considered a Hudswell, Clarke and Rodgers 1879-built 0-4-0 saddle tank situated at the Bute Works Supply Company of Cardiff (and recently back from completing a contract on the Orkney Islands). The inspection at the GWR shed Canton, Cardiff revealed that she was in poor condition and so the engine was not bought. The second locomotive considered was sited at Richborough and after negotiations a price of £1,600 was agreed upon but the deal fell through. The locomotive was possibly a small railmotor 2-2-0 tank of the LSWR class 'C4' No. 740, built at Nine Elms in 1906. Two further offers in 1920 were considered, one from T.W. Ward Ltd and the other from F. Wake but both were refused and so the search for new locomotives seemed to peter out.

If any of these locomotives had been successful, particularly if the problem with *Driver* had been discovered, before being broken up, then 'Jane' would not have been sent to Swindon in 1921, and would probably have been broken up!

All the company's engines were maintained on a daily service basis at Wantage Upper Yard shed which also had a small smithy and fitting shop. There was no machine shop equipment on site so heavy or complicated repairs were carried out at Swindon GWR Works or by the local engineers, The Wantage Engineering Co. Ltd.

Passenger Vehicles

As previously stated, Horse tramcars Nos. 1 and 2 were used as trailer passenger cars when steam was introduced to the line, both being taken out of service around 1913, but not scrapped until 1920.

In 1890, the company bought tramcar No. 3 from G.F. Milnes of Birkenhead (the successors to the Starbuck Car and Wagon Co.). This vehicle was able to seat about 20 passengers and survived right through until the withdrawal of passenger services and apparently it was still to been seen in a derelict state in the Upper Goods Yard in the 1930s.

On 30th July, 1903 the Wantage Tramway Co. purchased two tramcars from Reading Corporation. These were ex-horse tramcars Nos. 9 and 11 and cost eleven guineas and £16 5s. 6d. respectively. After arrival at Wantage they were renumbered to 4 and 5, with No. 4 (fomerly Reading Corporation's No. 11) being slightly larger thus the higher purchase price. The top decks were soon removed, and after the axleboxes and wheels were replaced by ex-GWR parts the vehicles were brought into use.

These converted coaches were not at all successful and appeared to be off the rails more than they were on them!. They were replaced in 1912 by two new cars from the Hurst Nelson & Co. Ltd of Motherwell, these also being numbered 4 and 5 by the tramway. No. 4 was a double deck open top bogie tramcar designed for electric traction which had been exhibited in London in 1900. As built, it had 68 passenger seats but before being sold to the WTC it was converted to a single deck vehicle for steam haulage and was equipped with steam heating. No. 5 had been built in 1904 as a railway carriage carrying 22 passengers for the Bradford Corporation, for use on their Nidd Valley Light Railway running from Lofthouse to Angram.

Locomotive No. 7 and passenger car No. 3 standing at the Mill Street terminus, Upper Yard in 1923. The gas holder can be seen in the background.

A.W. Croughton

Locomotive No. 7 on passenger duty, seen here standing on the spur (after the passing loop has been added) at the GWR Wantage Road Yard. Note the GWR signal box in the background.

LCGB, Ken Nunn Collection

Here locomotive No. 7 leaves the goods yard with at least a dozen assorted wagons. She is about to pass alongside 'The Volunteer' Inn on 17th June, 1939 *en route* for Wantage.   *H.C. Casserley*

The main road to Oxford from Wantage runs on the left and over the GWR railway bridge. The entrance from the road is into the GWR station goods yard, whilst the large white gateposts herald the track entrance of the Wantage Tramway into the goods yard and the terminus of the tramway. 'The Volunteer' Inn features on the extreme right, 11th October, 1930.

Dr Jack Hollick/Adrian Vaughan Collection

A view of the tramway terminus after closure, with a City of Oxford double-decker bus serving the station where once the tramway ran. This scene was captured on camera in March 1957.

H.C. Casserley

Locomotive No. 7, seen here with just three wagons having just left and passed 'The Volunteer' Inn, heads towards Wantage along the verge of the road near Grove Park Lodge in the 1930s.

K. Catchpole

About half a mile from the terminus, alongside the Lockinge Park, the Hughes tram engine No. 4 poses for a photograph on a sunny 1930s afternoon, with passenger cars No. 1 and 3 and conductor Savory (in uniform) in charge. *F.E.J. Burgiss*

Just beyond the location seen above, No. 7 heads a 'heavy' freight towards Wantage in June 1935, with the photographer's car in view. *H.C. Casserley*

The first bend encountered on the tramway after leaving the Wantage Road station terminus. Note how the track is virtually level with the road surface which caused all the problems during World War II, allowing the American vehicles to run over the track and also fling mud over it.
Real Photographs

The right-hand bend approaching Grove Farm. No. 7 (being overtaken by the cyclist) is struggling with eight freight wagons in the 1930s.
H.C. Casserley

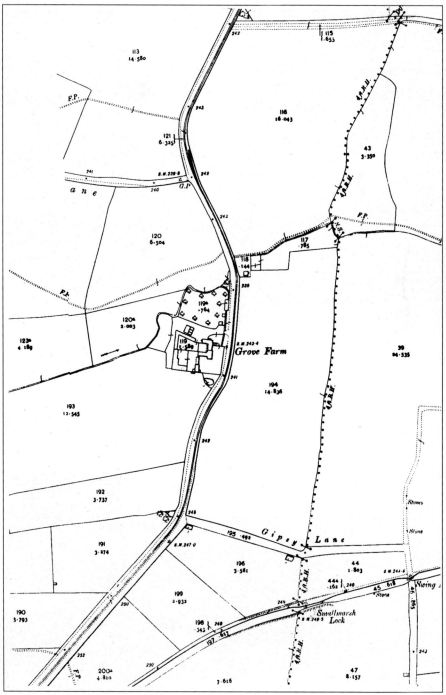

The tramway passing Grove farm.   *Reproduced from the 1906, 25 in. Ordnance Survey map.*

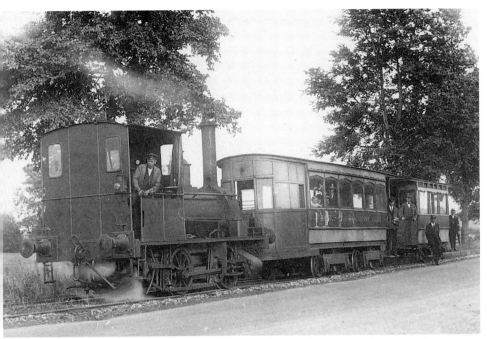

En route to the Wantage Road station terminus, No. 5 halts at the last official 'station' before the terminus, namely Oxford Lane. The siding at this point can be seen behind the engine amongst the long grass, 11th October, 1930.   *Dr Jack Hollick/Adrian Vaughan Collection*

A view of No. 7 near Grove on 21st May, 1937 on a long freight heading for Wantage Road station on a wet day.   *R.W. Kidner*

Locomotive No. 7 seen here hauling four box vans near Grove Park on a very wet day in the 1930s. These inclement days caused problems for the drivers because of the gradients and the poor state of the trackwork.
Howard Evans

An up goods passing 'Tenposts' on 10th May, 1930 with locomotive No. 5 hauling four wagons.
H.C. Casserley

cross it at Grove Street Crossing and enter onto company land, namely Palmers field. Just past the crossing, and on company land, was the site of a passing loop, removed in 1921. The main line ran straight on up a 1 in 47 gradient into 'The Cutting', whilst from a right-hand junction (just after Grove Street Crossing) another line curved away to the newer Lower Yard, so named simply because this yard was physically lower than the original Upper Station Yard. 'The Cutting' was in fact just a name for the section of track before the allotments were reached and then, subsequently, the station terminus.

At the time of the opening of the line, the terminus at the 'Upper Yard' consisted of a simple spur layout having just one passing loop; it was later changed to the one shown in the accompanying map. The facilities in the Upper Yard consisted of an undercover corrugated iron and wood passenger shed but at a later date a larger engine shed and repair shed was added, with half the structure being used as a goods shed. At the approach to the engine shed stood a timber-built coaling stage but this was too small for the purpose so coal was stacked (neatly) all around the area. The locomotive coal used originated from the Mountain Ash Colliery and was brought in by the GWR (via Wantage Road), the sand used in the locomotive sandboxes for wet weather adhesion was transported from a pit locally, near Frilford Heath, and brought to the site by horse and cart.

A yard crane standing near the engine shed was the only means of unloading heavy and bulky items on the line. A further small engine shed was added pre-1900 with an adjoining cattle dock. This shed stood over the Gas Works siding and the wagons for the gas works had to be pushed right through the shed before reaching the gas siding.

In 1904, the Tramway company's offices were constructed fronting onto Mill Street, Wantage, and these had an ornate brick frontage. The entrance to the Tramway's yard alongside these offices were guarded by large double wooden gates whilst a smaller wooden gate was used by employees of the nearby gas works.

The construction of a further branch line from the Grove Street Crossing direct into Clarks Flour Mill was considered, but this would have had to include a crossing of the busy Mill Street and it was eventually decided that this idea was not practical. Instead a modified version was implemented which terminated in a goods yard on the site of the old and derelict Wilts and Berks Canal wharf. This yard as previously mentioned, was known as Lower Yard, and commenced at the turn-out at Grove Street Crossing, proceeding westwards around Palmers Field, before turning south to run parallel to the main tramway line into the terminus. This yard was constructed in the early 1900s and opened officially on the 18th July, 1905, being better laid out than its counterpart, the original Upper Yard. Most of this new yard had been built on the old orchard of Mrs Langley which had been purchased for £1,000, together with parts on the old canal wharf site. Most of the freight traffic (which was steadily increasing) was handled by the Lower Yard. A small yard office and stables were erected by the Tramway company and their respective positions can be seen on the accompanying maps. The importance of Letcombe Brook was its use to water the company's horses stabled on the site. Coal was

On 17th June, 1939 locomotive No. 7 hauls a freight towards Wantage Lower Yard, and is seen here near Grove Wharf, next to the Wilts & Berks Canal. Note the lettering on the van in this train, 'Flour traffic only, empty to Wantage Road'.

H.C. Casserley

Passenger car No. 3 with tram engine No. 6 at Wantage terminus.   *F.E.J. Burgiss*

Passenger car No. 4 with locomotive No. 5 again at the terminus at Wantage. Note the poor state of repair of the engine shed roof.   *F.E.J. Burgiss*

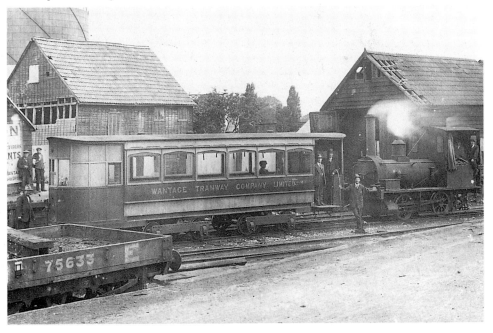

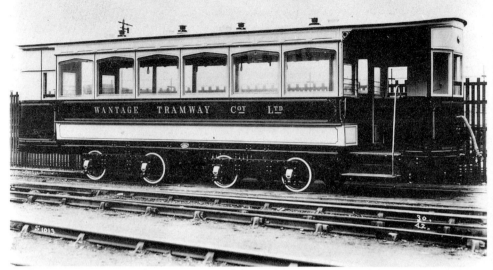

Passenger car No. 4 seen her in pristine condition in the yard at Hurst Nelson Company Works before delivery to the Wantage Tramway. Note the serif lettering.   *Courtesy Science Museum*

Passenger car No. 5 again as built at the Hurst Nelson Company Works. Note the ornate window frames.   *Courtesy Science Museum*

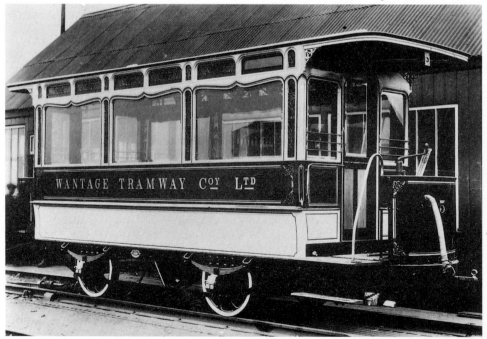

Passenger car No. 5 (an ex-Reading Tramways vehicle) seen here in 1905. Note the disc wheels used at this time.   *Lens of Sutton*

The Mathew's tram engine and passenger cars standing derelict in the Lower Yard orchard on 10th May, 1930.   *H.C. Casserley*

The layout at the GWR Wantage Road station before the quadrupling of the track in the 1930s. Note the station shunting horse posing with all the staff obviously during a lull in the main line traffic. Passengers entered the station under the canopy by the front door of the station master's house seen on the right, walked down the staircase past the station master's parlour, then onto the platform.

A view looking towards Paddington (east) showing the modernised station with the new up platform, road bridge and footbridge.   *British Railways*

Chapter Four

Description of the Route

In describing the route, a time period around 1930 has been adopted, as, in the life of the tramway many changes were implemented. The line commenced with a short siding within the confines of the Great Western Railway's station yard at Wantage Road station. This short spur lay parallel to the road and had a small passing loop (*see plan*) to allow a locomotive run-round, but there was no platform or cover for the passengers. Earlier only the spur existed, but in the line's closing years the layout was revised again and a through running line to the GWR sidings was laid.

Leaving Wantage Road on a short curve and passing 'The Volunteer' Inn, the tramway began a very-long straight run alongside the Wantage to Hanney road with the track tucked in beside the hedge on the roadside verge. The track ran alongside the Lockinge Estate and soon passed Grove Park Lodge. On the right-hand side, the fields became an Admiralty Depot during World War II. Nearing the first left-hand bend the route encountered Tulwick Lane which was passed on the left, and then, on the right a small copse called 'The Firs'. Just after the first left-hand bend, next to Oxford Lane on the right, was situated the first siding to be encountered on the line, used in the early days as a passenger stopping point.

The line continued on a slow curve to the right, passing a small thatched cottage called 'The Saltbox', which lay in a dip alongside the road. It is of note that the line had a sharp gradient (although short), in each direction at this point. The tramway continued to curve right past Grove Farm (situated on the right of the road and the line) and then on to Gypsy Lane, site of a loop which was in use in the early days of the tramway. A further long straight was encountered before reaching Canal cottages (this was where the Wilts and Berks Canal converged from the left), and then onto Grove Bridge itself. Just before the bridge was Grove siding, a single spur and the second 'station' on the line for passenger trains. The bridge itself was a substantial structure for such a tramway consisting of a 38 ft span over the canal (constructed of a steel girder) and was one of the major constructions on the tramway. It is interesting to note that the road alongside, crossed the Canal on a separate bridge.

Proceeding along towards Wantage, the tramway encountered another gradient and a left-hand bend as it neared Elms Farm. This farm was once named Godfreys Farm but in the middle of the 1930s became the main depot for Elm Farms Dairies. The route climbed yet again and had several small left and right bends before rounding a right-hand bend where Tenposts was reached. The line then ran in a straight line for a reasonable distance before entering a further right-hand bend opposite a large house called 'The Elms'. This residence boasted a garage very close to the road and with the tramway running alongside the road the tramway company had to provide a level crossing, which was of a very primitive nature.

The line then ran alongside the road until it bore left allowing the tramway to

A view of locomotive No. 4 with passenger car No. 3 (plus tramway staff and GWR staff) at the terminus spur of the Tramway at Wantage Road station about 1905. Note the GWR yard crane on the right which was used by the tramway and charged to their account. *Author's Collection*

A 1912 posed photograph of tram engine No. 6 and passenger car No. 4 again at the GWR Wantage Road terminus spur. Note the GWR goods shed in the background, on the right. The important passenger seems to have considerable luggage and could exceed his free allowance.
Chapman & Son

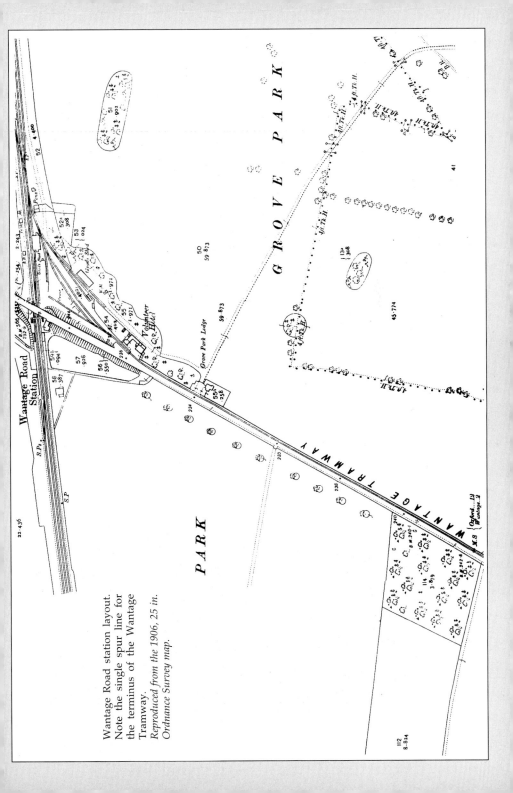

Wantage Road station layout. Note the single spur line for the terminus of the Wantage Tramway.
Reproduced from the 1906, 25 in. Ordnance Survey map.

A side view of tram engine No. 4 (designed by Henry Hughes of Loughborough in 1876 and built in 1882) at the Wantage Road terminus of the tramway, standing on the single road spur. Note that there is no platform or weather protection for the passengers.   *L&GRP*

The train in this view is made up in the same formation as the previous picture but this time the path from the road down to the 'station' can be seen, and also the GWR station master's house (*top right*).   *Lens of Sutton*

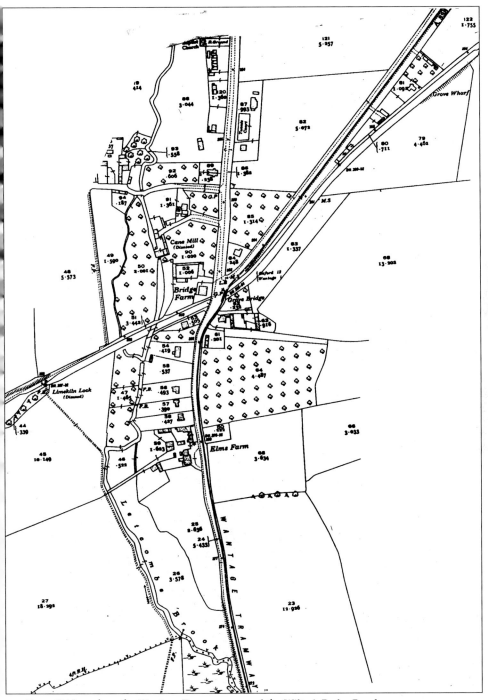

Grove Bridge where the Wantage Tramway crossed the Wilts & Berks Canal.
Reproduced from the 1906, 25 in. Ordnance Survey map.

Conductor Savory standing at Grove Bridge 'station' alongside the Hughes tram engine No. 4, and passenger cars No. 3 and 1. Note the siding alongside the main line.   *F.E.J. Burgiss*

A down train approaching Grove Bridge with locomotive No. 7 and passenger car No. 5. the photographer is standing on the canal bridge.   *Chapman & Son*

Another down service approaching Grove Bridge with competing traffic alongside. The Hughes tram engine No. 4 is hauling passenger cars No. 3, 1 and 4 (ex-Reading Tramways). Again photographed from the canal bridge, in 1905. *Real Photographs*

A view of the canal bridge at Grove (looking towards Wantage Road station), 11th October, 1930. *Dr Jack Hollick/Adrian Vaughan Collection*

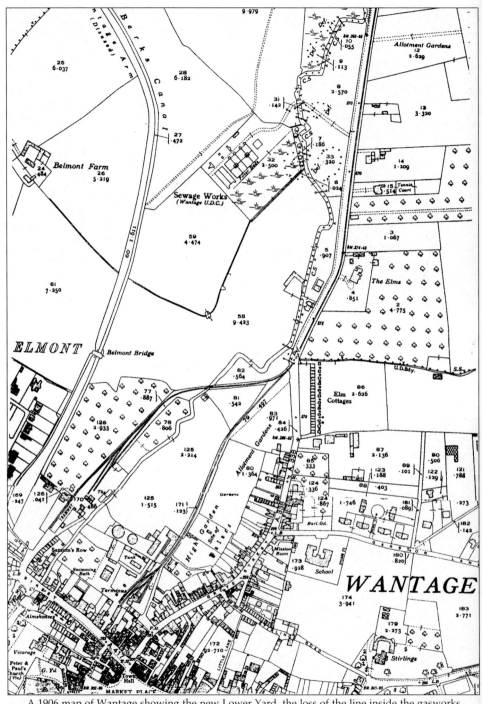

A 1906 map of Wantage showing the new Lower Yard, the loss of the line inside the gasworks and the new office buildings at the terminus.

Reproduced from the 1906, 25 in. Ordnance Survey map.

Standing on the trackbed, the photographer has depicted well the way the tramway line ran right alongside, and level with, the road and close to the fence. This view shows the track crossing Grove Road and entering into company land at Wantage. *Real Photographs*

A close-up look at the crossing and the important 'point' that allowed trains to the passenger terminus (*straight on*) and the line to the Lower Yard goods depot (*right*). Note the gas holder in the distance giving some idea of the distance to the terminus, 11th October, 1930.

Dr Jack Hollick/Adrian Vaughan Collection

A fine view of No. 7 crossing the main Oxford to Wantage road with a freight train from Wantage Road to the Lower Yard on 17th June, 1939. Note the very large 'Level Crossing' notice boards for road traffic, that faced each way, as there were no gates or traffic signals.

H.C. Casserley

No. 5 (nicknamed 'Jane') running in its 80th year, lurks in the back alleyways of Wantage in 1936.

Dr I.C. Allen

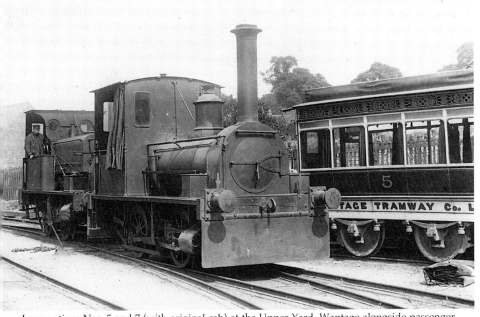

Locomotives Nos. 5 and 7 (with original cab) at the Upper Yard, Wantage alongside passenger car No. 5.
Author's Collection

A further Upper Yard scene with passenger cars No. 3 and 5 (in the non-serif livery) with steam tram No. 6.
Courtesy Science Museum

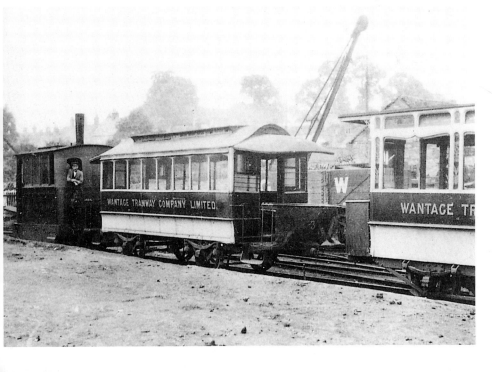

Looking north towards the throat of Wantage Upper Yard, 11th October, 1930.

Dr Jack Hollick/Adrian Vaughan Collection

Locomotive No. 7 shunting several Eckington Private Owner wagons in the upper terminus yard, alongside the 1894 engine shed (the line through this shed went to the town gasworks sidings) photographed in 1939. *H.C. Casserley*

An 'officially' posed photograph of the staff at Wantage Upper Yard terminus around 1892 prior to the new engine shed being built). Locomotive No. 5 (with its customary two truck load for that period) stands on the goods spur whilst the town gasworks can be seen in the background. Note the Private Owner wagon for Clarke and Sons, Town Mills, Wantage.

Author's Collection

A good view of the track layout at the Wantage terminus on 11th October, 1930 with the yard crane (*left*), the workshop and engine shed (*middle*), the old terminus buildings, now car garages, and the 'new' 1894 engine shed (*extreme right*).   *Dr Jack Hollick/Adrian Vaughan Collection*

Another view of the town terminus on the same day. The former terminus buildings are now in a derelict state and are converted into garages. A very sorry-looking passenger car No. 3 lies at the end of line whilst three Private Owner wagons belonging to Langford's of Abingdon wait to be unloaded nearby.   *Dr Jack Hollick/Adrian Vaughan Collection*

Viewed from the station yard is the old covered terminus platform at Wantage, Mill Street. Note the crude supports wedged to the uprights to help support the canopy.   *F.E.J. Burgiss*

A further view of the under-cover platform area with steam tram No. 6 on duty.
Author's Collection

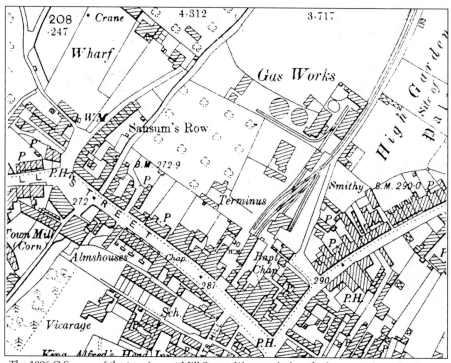

The 1896 O.S. map of the terminus at Mill Street, Wantage before the lower yard was built.
Reproduced from the 1896, 25 in. Ordnance Survey map.

Looking up Mill Street, Wantage (towards the Market Place) with the 1904 Wantage Tramway offices on the left and the gate into the station yard just below. *Author's Collection*

The Tramway Terminus and
Mill Street, Wantage.

No. 7 travelling light engine on its way to the Lower Yard on 17th June, 1939. This appears to be the only photograph ever taken on this part of the line. *H.C. Casserley*

A line up of the tramway's horse-drawn fleet in Lower Yard, photographed in the early 1900s. The stables are on the right, whilst, in the background, the yard seems full of wagons which are loaded or being unloaded; a very busy scene indeed. *Author's Collection*

collected from the Lower Yard by Pates Coal Merchants although the main coal merchants operated from the Upper Yard.

With Clark's Mill nearby, flour was a constant merchandise being manhandled in the Lower Yard. It was a recognised fact that Berkshire wheat was particularly suitable for biscuit making and so much of the flour from the town mill was despatched to the well-known biscuit companies of the time.

A pocket timetable of 1900.   *Author*

Chapter Five

Day to Day Running of the Tramway, 1875-1925

Before 1900, the company had enjoyed steady growth and stability under the managerial skills of Mr Aldworth and Mr Watson. Its shareholders were receiving a regular dividend of around 4 per cent and the public were, to all accord, pleased with the passenger service provided. The timetable for the early years was as follows:

		November, 1879		
Leave Wantage	*Down GWR Trains*	*Leave Wantage*	*Up GWR Trains*	
9.25 am for the	9.48	7.05 am for the	7.30	
12.08 pm	1.06	9.25	10.07	
12.40	1.06 (Wed.)	12.08 pm	12.33	
5.25	5.50	2.17	2.42	
8.20	8.45	6.05	6.28	

At the turn of the century, the service was worked so that the Tramway trains met every GWR stopping train at Wantage Road on weekdays but not on Sundays. It was also the policy of the company to meet any excursion train that stopped and also run extra services on Market days. Whenever the GWR changed its timetable, so did the tramway, to suit.

		1905, Summer		
Leave Wantage	*Down GWR Trains*	*Leave Wantage*	*Up GWR Trains*	
7.40 am for the	8.05	7.05 am for the	7.29	
9.15	9.45	9.35	9.59	
(Slip Coach Daily)	10.30	11.00	11.34	
11.00	11.22	12.05 pm	12.31	
1.25 pm	1.48	2.25	2.50	
3.10	3.35	6.15	6.39	
5.35	6.00	7.50	8.15	
6.30	6.56			
7.50	8.52			
8.30	8.52 (Sats.)			

The above timetable was probably the 'heaviest' work-load the tramway operated.

During 1900 a further local railway was mooted by Mr Hassard (under the newly passed Light Railway Act) from Lambourn to Abingdon with running powers over the Wantage Tramway, but this did not materialise as all parties concerned felt it unlikely to succeed.

Fares on the tramway at this time were always higher than those of other urban tramways, but passengers' luggage was carried free of charge on the platform end of each of the vehicles. In addition, the company undertook to deliver or collect luggage in Wantage for just a few pence payment.

First and second class compartments were maintained during the early years

EMPIRE THEATRE,

SWINDON,

Thursday, March 11th.

'SUCCESSFUL MUSICAL COMEDY

THE CATCH OF THE SEASON

Cheap Tram, Rail and Reserved Theatre Seat at an inclusive price of

4/4

leaving by the 5.35 p.m. Car, returning from Swindon 11.10 p.m.

SEATS MUST BE BOOKED EARLY.

W. NOBLE.

GIBBS, PRINTER, WANTAGE.

An inclusive all-in price of 4s. 4d. for the tram, the GWR to Swindon and the ticket to the theatre is offered in this poster by the Wantage Tramway Co. The exact date is unknown but the train times first appeared in the 1905 timetable.   *Author's Collection*

of the service and tickets were issued accordingly until 1st January, 1889, after which date the first class was abandoned and a uniform fare was introduced.

Single Fares	1875-1888		1889
	1st class	2nd class	(One class)
Wantage/Grove Bridge	4d.	3d.	2d.
Wantage/Oxford Lane	6d.	4½d.	4d.
Wantage/Wantage Road	9d.	6d.	6d.

By 1903, with the new General Manager, Mr W.A. Noble and his goods manager, Mr J. Bullock, the tramway enjoyed a period of true expansion. Early in 1904 a new office building at Mill Street, Wantage was erected to deal with this. It cost £240 and was constructed as an extension to the existing station house, which dated from 1876. The building consisted of two storeys with a very ornate terra-cotta frontage. The manager's office was situated on the first floor with the general office below incorporating a small travel service counter for the general public. The old station building contained a waiting room and parcel office and an entry to the station's covered platform. During 1904 the new Lower Yard branch was constructed (using Krupp's steel rail purchased second-hand from the MSWJ and laid by the Tramway's own staff), being officially opened on the 1st July, 1905.

The 15th February, 1909 saw an unusual and interesting event in the life of the Wantage Tramway when a train of eight SECR four-wheeled passenger coaches (carrying over 160 military personnel) worked over the Tramway, conveying Lieut Napier Burnett Lindsay's funeral train to the Lower Yard at Wantage. He had been fatally wounded in a hunting accident at Aldershot on February 11th. Apparently the couplings of the train had to be loosened to accommodate the tight curves of the Tramway and a second engine followed the train in case assistance was needed (but this proved to be unnecessary).

Passengers carryings during these early years were as follows (each survey being dated at the 30th September):

1895	36,692	1903	45,438
1899	37,609	1904	50,627
1900	39,044	1905	54,976
1902	43,678	1906	56,180

During 1904 over 3,600 truck loads were received via the GWR and by 1911 this load figure had topped the 5,700 mark.

After the outbreak of World War I, the line suffered considerably from the loss of the horse racing trade from around the area, plus the strain of the military requirements enforced on the Tramway. Fares and freight charges had to be increased and to crown it all, the all important flour mill had to be closed.

Peace time regrettably did not bring an immediate return to prosperity and it is probably safe to say that the tramway never fully recovered from the effects of World War I. Maintenance of the rolling stock had been neglected and the company found itself desperately in need of a 'goods' engine and, as previously mentioned, a Manning, Wardle 0-4-0 engine named *The Driver* was hurriedly purchased from the Woolwich Arsenal for £600.

To add to the Tramway's already mounting troubles, the Manager, Mr W.A. Noble turned out to be less illustrious than his name implied. In November 1919, after 20 years of apparently dedicated service Mr Noble left his job and fled the area to escape the consequences of swindling the Tramway Company out of an estimated £1,000. Although this event brought about a general tightening up of the company's affairs, it left the tramway without a full time manager until January 1922. The post was then filled by Joe Bullock a one-time clerk to the tramway, who had left its service a few years previously to manage the Langford's Coal and Corn Company. However because of Langford's dealings with the Tramway and the fact that the depot was right next to the terminus, he had not lost touch with his old employers and was well-informed to deal with the problems he inherited.

By 1923 the fares for the one-class service were:

Wantage to Grove Bridge	3*d.*
Wantage to Oxford Lane	6*d.*
Wantage to GWR Wantage Rd	9*d.*

1923, Summer

Leave Wantage		*Down GWR Trains*		*Leave Wantage*		*Up GWR Trains*	
7.08	am for the	8.02		7.08	am for the	7.30	
9.30		9.47		8.10		8.34	
10.25		10.44		9.30		10.09	(Mon.)
12.10	pm	12.38		9.48		10.09	(Tue., Wed.,
		& 12.43	(Mon.)				Thu., Fri., Sat.)
12.15		12.38	(Tue, Wed.,12.10 pm		12.25	(Mon.)
		& 12.43	Thu., Fri.,	12.05		12.25	(Tue., Wed.,
			Sat.)				Thu., Fri., Sat.)
3.15		3.37		2.20		2.43	
5.40		6.02		6.32		6.55	
8.18		8.37		7.35		7.59	

The new appointment brought an improvement in the goods traffic, but receipts from the passenger service continued to show a gradual decline. This was due to a number of factors but the greatest influence was the introduction by the GWR in 1924 of an omnibus service which took in Wantage and the surrounding villages and later included the route between Wantage Road Station and the town.

The situation did not improve and after careful consideration the Directors decided to close down the passenger service. The last run took place on the evening of 31st July, 1925 and scores of people waited at the Grove Street Crossing to pile on board the tramcars for the short run up to the terminus. The detonators which exploded on the line and the cheers of the crowd on the platform marked the end of an eventful half-century in British transport history.

A summary of the company's passenger, parcel and goods income from 1917 to 1925 is listed opposite;

Year ending 30th Sept.	Passengers £	Parcels £	Goods £
1917	977	220 †	1667
1918	1619	246 †	1820
1919	1863	205	1539
1920	not known		
1921	1617	252	3959
1922	not known		
1923	1538	421	3737
1924	1481	416	3607
1925	928 *	356 *	3125

† Including mails.   * Until 31st July only.

A track level photograph of the covered platform terminus at Wantage.

Courtesy Science Museum

Locomotive No. 7 hauling No. 5 (dead) along Wantage Road past 'The Volunteer' Inn for the last time in May 1946 *en route* to the GWR yard and then to Swindon Works.   *Oakwood Collection*

A last farewell to No. 5 with its coupling rods removed as it leaves the GWR Wantage Road goods yard marshalled in a pick up goods train on its way to the GWR Works at Swindon for preservation.   *Oakwood Collection*

Chapter Six

Freight Only and Closure

With the cessation of traffic and the parcel traffic virtually non existent, the company faced a crisis and had to find ways of reducing running costs. The first to suffer were the staff, who were trimmed back, and as a result the office accommodation at the Mill Street offices became redundant and was leased out. The small amount of clerical work which remained was carried out in a small shed in the Lower Yard. By 1929, the post of Manager was discontinued and Mr Bullock left the company.

The tramway now concentrated on goods and mineral traffic, with most of the trade coming from Clark's Mill. During this time and right up to closure the tramway made a yearly profit and also paid a dividend. This was in spite of the fact that the line and its equipment were rapidly falling into disrepair and no maintenance was being carried out.

The freight service being provided was reasonable and mostly ran on time as follows: an 8 am goods down to the GWR Wantage Road station; a further service at around 11 am and the last run about 4 pm, (this after an afternoon's shunting in the Lower Yard). The whole of this service was handled throughout this period of time by just two locomotives, No. 5 and No. 7, with an average load of five wagons per trip.

As the tramway entered World War II period, it had just 13 full time employees. Little effect was felt at first, but as the war progressed petrol became scarce and the Tramway began to increase its loadings. This renewed prosperity was unfortunately short-lived as, by 1943, the Americans (who were based nearby at Grove) had vandalised the track by churning up the mud and also running over parts of the track with heavy vehicles. The tramway was completely out of action for three months with a fierce argument going on as to the responsibility for the problem. In the end the Americans refused to pay any compensation but agreed to clear up the mud. This and the closing of the gas works (which had produced a healthy and regular revenue for the tramway) made the decision to close the system inevitable.

By December 1945, the only locomotive in service was No. 7, but when it was inspected by the GWR the locomotive was more or less written off: 'completely worn out' was the wording on the report.

The last offical trip over the whole length of the line took place on 21st December, 1945 a little over 70 years after the first horse-drawn service on the Tramway. In 1946, the properties were auctioned with the plant and machinery being sold on 25th April. One of the items in that sale was 5,170 yards of track, and locomotive No. 7 was sold for £205 to A.R. Adams of Newport, Monmouthshire, under the condition that she remained on the Tramway until the end and could be used in the dismantling and lifting operations.

This operation commenced in May 1946, with No. 7 taking all the scrap down to the GWR yard at Wantage Road station in small loads. (With the whole job finalised, locomotive No. 7 then left by road to her new owner in Wales.)

With assets of over £10,000, the preference share holders were paid up in full, and the ordinary shareholders were paid £3 12s. 11½d. each.   A final shareholders' meeting was held on 15th April, 1947 and the company was dissolved on 18th July, 1947.

So ended the Wantage Tramway Company.

The fate of *Shannon* has already been recorded in *Chapter Three*.

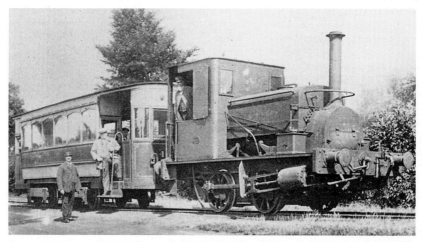

Lone passenger car No. 4, is formed behind locomotive No. 7, as it pauses at Grove Bridge 'station' in 1914.   *Chapman & Sons*

Chapter Seven

Working on the Tramway

Although a vast number of technical and descriptive articles have been written about the Wantage Tramway for magazines and newspapers, there have been very few attempts to record life as an employee of the company. Fortunately one of the best accounts was written in 1973 by 70-year-old Leslie Belcher. Entitled 'My Memoirs' it was published in the form of a pamphlet by the Wantage Museum Committee and it recorded his memories of almost 30 years during which he worked on the tramway.

Les Belcher started as a parcels boy for the company in 1916 at the age of 13. As the first tram was due out just after seven o'clock he had to be on duty by 6.45 am to open the parcels room and see that everything was loaded onto the tram.

The next job of the day, and possibly the most important, was to take a can from the manager's office and collect half-a-pint of milk from Simmonds Dairy in Grove Street. This had to be ready for the Manager when he returned from his daily inspection of the Lower Yard.

After this Les had to clean the platform, the toilets, the waiting room and the offices. He finished in time to unload the tram which had returned from Wantage Road station carrying fish, meat, mail, newspapers and parcels in addition to passengers with their luggage.

The incoming goods had to be sorted out - some for delivery around the town and some to await collection by people who lived in surrounding villages. The latter were advised by post that goods awaited collection and they usually arranged for them to be picked up by carriers who called at Wantage two or three times a week.

A charge was made for the collection or delivery of luggage. When Les first started work the charge was 2d. to have an article delivered to a destination within 300 yds of the tramway office, or 3d. if the distance was more than 300 yds. Later the charges were increased to '. . within 200 yds.- 3d. per article, up to 500 yds - 4d.; and more than 500 yds - 6d.' Receipts were issued but in the latter years of the passenger service the parcels boy was allowed to pocket the money if the delivery was made after 9 pm!

As a parcels boy Les earned about six shillings a week and for that he often had to work until 10 pm. Fortunately the customers were generous with their tips and most weeks he made more from tips than he was paid in wages.

Commercial travellers nearly always gave good tips. They arrived on the tram with skips of samples to show the shopkeepers, and Les had to load them onto a sack truck and trundle them around to the different shops. At the end of the day he had to take the skips back to the tramway station in time to catch the 5.30 pm tram to Wantage Road

When he became too old for the job of parcels boy Les worked on platform duties for a short time, then he was moved to the goods office at the Lower Yard. As well as office work he was expected to help with jobs such as roping and sheeting wagons, loading empty crates and shunting.

There was a considerable reduction in the number of employees when the passenger service ceased, but Les was kept on and moved to Wantage Road station where he worked as a checker for the Tramway company. He stayed there until the tramway closed and he was given an extra five pounds in his wages together with a letter of thanks for his services when he was finally paid off in December 1945.

Les kept one or two relics of his years with the tramway but he regretted the day in 1945 when he was told to make a bonfire of some of the company's paperwork because it was rumoured that the tramway was about to close. The cash books, letters, ticket books and way bills that went up in flames would have been worth their weight in gold to local historians today!

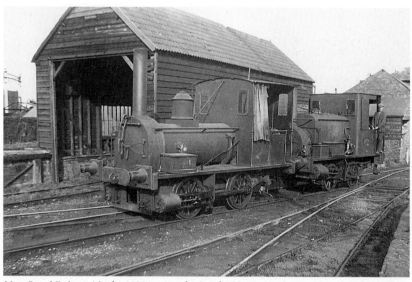

Nos. 5 and 7 alongside the 1894 engine shed at the Upper Yard, Wantage on 11th October, 1930. Note the gasworks which can just be seen in the background on the far left.
Dr Jack Hollick/Adrian Vaughan Collection

Appendix One

Chronology

22nd Oct., 1873	A meeting of persons favourable to a tramway communication between Wantage and Wantage Road station held at the Town Hall, Wantage
10th Nov., 1873	The Wantage Tramway Company Ltd incorporated
9th March, 1874	First General Meeting of the Shareholders
7th August, 1874	Act confirming the Wantage Provisional Order received the Royal Assent (37 & 38 Vict. c. 183)
26th Aug., 1875	Col Hutchinson, RE, inspected the Tramway on behalf of the Board of Trade
1st Oct., 1875	The Tramway Company commenced a goods service (by road), as agents to the GWR
11th Oct., 1875	The Tramway opened for passenger traffic
27th June, 1876	Act to amend the Wantage Tramways Order, 1874, received the Royal Assent (39 & 40 Vict. c. 42). Mechanical traction authorised subject to Board of Trade regulations (*vide* 1st February, 1877)
1st August, 1876	Steam traction introduced for passenger traffic
25th Nov., 1876	Col Hutchinson, RE, inspected the Grantham steam car and the Merryweather tram engine
1st Feb., 1877	The Board of Trade Byelaws governing the use of steam came into force
24th Mar., 1877	Visit to the Wantage Tramway of members of the Select Committee of the House of Commons on the use of Mechanical Power on Tramways
c. December 1878	The Tramway in working order for heavy goods
March 1879	The General Manager of the GWR (Mr Grierson) declined to undertake the working of the tramway
August to Nov. 1880	Trials with two Mekarski compressed air engines
1st Jan., 1889	First and second class abandoned, and a uniform fare adopted
During 1900	Proposal for a light railway from Lambourn to Abingdon, with running powers over the Wantage Tramway
1st July, 1905	Branch to the Lower Goods Yard opened
10th Feb., 1920	A new Board of Directors appointed
During 1920	Lt-Col H.S. Stephens became interested in the tramway
31st July, 1925	Last day of the passenger service
During 1936	The GWR declined to take over the Tramway
15th Nov., 1943 to 14th Feb., 1944 (*both dates inclusive*)	Line temporarily closed
18th Dec., 1945	Last day of normal traffic
21st Dec., 1945	Last day of traffic outwards service only
25th April, 1946	Sale of the company's plant and equipment
During 1946	Dismantling of the line
12th Nov. 1946	Last Annual General Meeting of the Shareholders
15th April, 1947	Final meeting of Shareholders
18th July, 1947	The company was deemed to be dissolved

Locomotive No. 7 near Grove Wharf with a heavy freight load on 17th June, 1939.

H.C. Casserley

Another long freight with No. 7 again in charge. The alternative form of transport then becoming established as a replacement to the tramway can be seen on the road.

Peter Johnson Collection

Appendix Two

Tickets

The Wantage tramway tickets were always printed by local printing companies and were of just two types. Those of the first type, were printed on sheets of card which were cut up by hand when necessary and were in circulation for at least three years. They were quite plain in style and the first class tickets had their lettering in black whilst the second class had the type in orange print. Headed 'Wantage Tramway', they stated the destination from Wantage, the fare and the class only. Being hand cut size varied slightly but they were intended to be 3 in. x 1½ in. Tickets of the second style were printed on thin paper and headed 'Wantage Tramway Company' or 'Wantage Tramway Co. Ltd.' with the fare only and no destination. However as can be seen by the samples the heading and the fare were rendered more or less insignificant by the advertisements of the town's business enterprises covering most of the front and all of the back of each ticket. Again their size varied between 4½ in. x 2¾ in. and 4¾ in. x 2½ in. and they were issued in books of 250. Initially all were white but in later printings each individual fare stage was allocated a different colour. These appeared to have been introduced around September 1879 as the half-yearly accounts incorporated an entry for revenue from advertising on tickets.

As far as can be ascertained the tickets were issued and collected by the travelling conductor but the through tickets to include the GWR services were issued at the Mill Street offices and the tramway received a 2½ per cent commission on receipts. It appears that the conductor stood by a table just inside the passenger car's body right next to the end-platform entrance, where he took the money and issued the tickets. When the passengers alighted they placed their tickets in a box provided - again near the coach platform-end.

The original concept of the early days of travelling on the Tramway for a penny a mile never really materialised and the following fares were set at the time of opening the line:

	Single		Return	
	1st	2nd	1st	2nd
From Wantage to Wantage Road Stn or back.	9d.	6d.	1s. 3d.	10d.
From Wantage to Oxford Lane or GWR Stn to Grove Canal Bridge	6d.	4½d.	10d.	8d.
From Wantage to Grove Bridge or GWR Stn to Oxford Lane	4d.	3d.	6d.	4½d.

The above prices included the carriage of 112lb. of baggage free for first class passengers and 56lb. worth in weight for the second class passengers. It had been intended that a third class fare would be available but this was abandoned before the opening of the line. The fares would have been;

Wantage to Wantage Road GWR	4d. (return 7d.)
Wantage to Grove Bridge	2d. (return 3d.)
Wantage to Oxford Lane	3d. (return 5d.)

As from January 1889, a uniform rate and class was adopted and this lead to the whole journey costing 6d.; Grove Bridge to Wantage costing 2d. and Oxford Lane to Wantage 4d. Several special fares were in operation, such as a weekly

93

workman's return ticket for 2s. 6d., quarterly tickets for 32s. 6d. and free passes for company staff* with special reductions for local tradesmen connected or advertising with the Tramway. Children under three travelled free and those between 3 and 12 years old were charged half fare.

The fares for the tramway just before passenger closure were:

FARES
From the Timetable for 9th July, 1923

Wantage to Wantage Road	9d.	Market Tickets
" Grove Bridge	3d.	Wednesday
' Oxford Lane	6d.	and
" Wantage Road and		Saturday
back by same car	9d.	Return Fares
Children under 3 years Free, above 3		Wantage Rd. to Wantage 1s.
and under 12 Half-price.		Oxford Lane to Wantage 9d.
Bicycles and Perambulators accom-		Grove Bridge to Wantage 4d.
panying Passengers 6d. each.		

* Free passes were available to employees of the Tramway company and their wives, the GWR station master at Wantage Road station, together with the booking clerk, porters and their wives, signalmen and their wives and also Mr Sims and his wife from 'The Volunteer' Inn. Mr Ireson from Wantage Road (contractor at the GWR Wantage Road Goods Yard) also held a free pass.

These tickets were printed locally, probably by J. Lewis & Co. (predecessor of Clegg & Son). Each of the tickets around the circle had a letter in the top left-hand corner. The numbers after this usually ranged between 1 and 50. The letters corresponded to the following fare stages:

A Wantage to Grove Bridge *Single*   G Wantage Road to Oxford Lane *Single*
B Wantage to Grove Bridge *Return*   H Wantage Road to Oxford Lane *Return*
C Wantage to Oxford Lane *Single*   I Wantage Road to *
D Wantage to Oxford Lane *Return*   K Wantage Road to *
E Wantage to Wantage Road *Single*   L Wantage Road to *
F Wantage to Wantage Road *Return*   M Wantage Road to *

* The use of letters,I, K, L, M, varies slightly according to class.

Appendix Three

Staff and Salaries

William Stevenson, son of the Company Engineer was made a part-time manager in April 1876 at a salary of £25 per year. The post was made permanent when, in October 1877, Mr J.G. Spencer was appointed as Manager at a salary of £75 per annum. Several other Managers came and went but there is no record of their salaries until the notorious N.A. Noble arrived on the scene at a salary of £110 per year. This appointment proved useful during Noble's office as considerable equipment was purchased, (very reasonably priced), from Noble's previous employer, the MSWJ railway, where he had been in charge of the goods service at Cirencester. As previously recorded Mr Noble left suddenly under suspicion of fraud. In 1920, Mr H.H. Turner (a GWR station master from Wheatley in Oxfordshire) held the post of Manager for a limited time until eventually Mr J. Bullock was appointed to the post from the 1st January, 1922 at a salary of £325 per annum.

The train conductor's salaries in 1885 were just 10s. per week but by 1887 had been raised to 12s. per week, in 1888 to 13s. per week and in 1892 to 14s. per week.

The parcels boy at the terminus station in Mill Street, Wantage received only 5s. per week and although this was a low wage he did manage to pick up numerous tips to supplement his wages. In fact it was rumoured that there was a long waiting list for the post as this lad was one of the best paid on the railway! The following wages were recorded in the pay sheets depicting weekly pay in 1903:

Manager 50s.; Clerk 30s.; Engineer 36s.; Ganger 30s.; Driver 24s.; Conductor 17s. 6d.; Shunter 17s.; and Parcel Officer 6s.

Bibliography

Various documents relating to the Wantage Tramway can be seen in railway museums and local museums, and a good deal of material is available at Berkshire Record Office, also the Bodleian Library, Oxford, County Record Office, Oxford, the House of Lords Record Office, and the Public Record Office, Kew. In addition the articles and books listed below were a great help to the author of this book. They can easily be obtained by anyone who is really interested in pursuing the history of the tramway.

Articles
(1) 'The Wantage Tramway', by T.R. Perkins & F. Merton Atkins.
     Railway Magazine, September, 1928.
(2) Letter by R.L.P. Jowitt and Editorial, *The Times*, 8th April, 1946.
     Subsequent letters, *The Times*, 11th, 12th & 18th April and 6th May, 1946.
(3) 'The Wantage Tramway', by M.E.J. Deane
     Model Railway News, March, 1963.
(4) 'Recollections of the Wantage Tramway', by John Pope.
     Railway World, December, 1965.
(5) Various references. *Great Western Echo* - (Magazine of the Great Western Society.) Spring Issue 1969 to Autumn Issue 1973.
(6) 'JANE', by K. Greenhalgh, M. Williams and L. Elias.
     Harlequin - Leisure Magazine of A.E.R.E. Harwell, Summer Issue 1969.
(7) 'The Tramway Centenary', by L.A. Summers
     North Berks Herald, 18th October, 1973.

Books
(1) *The Wantage Tramway*, by S.H. Pearce Higgins.
     Abbey Press, 1958.
(2) *History of the Steam Tram*, by H.A. Whitcombe.
     Oakwood Press, 1961.
(3) *Victorian Wantage*, by Kathleen Philip.
     Published by the author, 1968.
(4) *Minor Railways of England and their Locos 1900-1939*
     Goose & Sons, Norwich, 1970.
(5) *The Cromford & High Peak Railway*, by A. Rimmer
     Oakwood Press, 1971.
(6) *The Wilts & Berks Canal*, by L.J. Dalby.
     Oakwood Press, 1971, Second Edition, 1986.
(7) *My Memoirs*, by Leslie Belcher
     Wantage Museum Committee, 1973.
(8) *The Wantage Tramway*, by Nicholas De Courtais.
     Wild Swan Publications, 1981.